— THE GOURMET KITCHEN —

CHILES & OTHER PEPPERS

WRITTEN BY JOHANNA YOUNGER & JAMES FISHER
ILLUSTRATED BY JANE BREWSTER

SUNSET PUBLISHING CORPORATION
MENLO PARK, CALIFORNIA

A QUARTO BOOK

Library of Congress Catalog Card Number: 94-66125

ISBN 0-376-02761-4

This book was designed and produced by
Quarto Inc.
The Old Brewery, 6 Blundell Street
London N7 9BH

Editors: Kate Kirby, Laura Washburn, Susan Ward
Art Editor: Mark Stevens
Designer: Julie Francis
Art Director: Moira Clinch
Editorial Director: Sophie Collins

First published in North America in 1994 by Sunset Publishing Corporation
Menlo Park, CA 94025

First Sunset printing September 1994

Typeset in Great Britain by Central Southern Typesetters, Eastbourne, UK
Manufactured in Singapore by Bright Arts Pte. Ltd.
Printed in China by Leefung-Asco Printers Ltd.

Contents

Introduction

Chile peppers are essential to many cultures and religions; they have been worshipped, used medicinally, and even employed as an insecticide. In ancient civilizations, and indeed in many developing countries today, chiles are used to ward off evil spirits and bring well-being into the home. But most of all, chiles are used to season the cuisines of the world.

The Americas are blessed with myriad chiles, from small, pointed, and hot, to large, round, and mild. Some of the world's hottest chiles go into Mexican *salsas* and Peruvian side dishes.

In the marketplaces of Asia, merchants trade in chiles as in stocks and bonds; people buy sackfuls of chiles that would last a Westerner a lifetime. Thai food vendors steam and fry pungent, spicy foods in the streets. Malaysians peddle bowls of chile noodles and hot prawn or chicken satay from mobile kitchens perched on bicycles. The curries, masalas, tandooris, and marinades of India are spiced with chiles, ranging from searingly hot in the south to mild in the north.

North Africans make fiery *harissa* sauce from chiles pounded with spices, such as cumin, coriander, cinnamon, and caraway,

while their spicy salads give new meaning to the word hot. In southern and eastern Europe, milder sweet chile peppers are used in stews, sauces, and seasonings.

Archeologists tell us that chiles — probably wild — were eaten in Mexico from as early as 7000BC; 4500 years later they became some of the earliest cultivated plants. Chiles were an integral part of life for the Incas, Aztecs, and Mayans, who used them in cooking, medicines, and spiritual preparations. Chiles were used, maybe even cultivated, by ancestors of the Pueblo Indians 1000 years before Spanish colonization.

When Christopher Columbus arrived in the West Indies in 1492, he also found chiles. Believing they were peppers (*Piper nigrum*), he shipped the seeds back to Spain. From there, chiles spread like fire through the rest of Europe and, via the

Portuguese spice routes, to Asia and Africa. Strangely, chiles didn't arrive in the American South, despite the proximity to their origin, until they had circumnavigated the globe. It was the Europeans who brought chiles to feed their African slaves. Just 100 years after Columbus' discoveries, the fiery fruits had conquered the hearts and tastes of nations. Today chiles are still the most widely used flavoring in the world.

Varieties of Chiles

There are about 200 different types of chiles – you'll find them fat, skinny, round, or pointed; red, yellow, purple, brown, white and green. Some are mildly sweet and others have vicious tempers; some taste bitter, others pungent. There are chiles that are aptly named, descriptively named, or deceptively named. They are sold fresh, dried, smoked, or marinated. All, however,

are genus *Capsicum,* which includes bell peppers and paprikas. Chiles and bell peppers are fruits, but we tend to think of them as vegetables; dried and ground, we call them spice. Members of the nightshade family, they are related to the potato, the tomato, and tobacco. Chiles are rich in vitamin C, have a moderate level of vitamins A – more in red fruits than in green – and E, but are low in calories and fat.

Some chiles are indigenous to certain parts of the world and exhibit certain characteristics, depending on where they are grown. The Spanish now market *denomination controlée* peppers, named after the region in which they are grown, rather than the variety.

What all chiles have in common is *capsaicin,* the oily substance found in the ribs near the seed heart, giving the chile its heat. Seeds taste hot because of their proximity to the veins. Removing both seeds and veins before cooking can reduce the heat. The degree of heat is not necessarily related to chile size, but often, the smaller the fruit, the hotter its bite! The level of *capsaicin* can be affected by growing conditions — you will find the hotter chiles in hot and arid countries. In any case, more mature chiles are sweeter.

Measuring the heat in chiles is extremely difficult. One method computes chile heat on a scale ranging from 1 to 10. The following list includes the more commonly used peppers and their relative heat as computed on that scale.

Ají This is the South American term for chile peppers. *Ají panca,* red or purple chiles, are used fresh and dried in Peruvian cooking; and *ají mirasol,* which means "look at the sun," are dried, usually deep yellow to red chiles used in *moles, seviche,* and *salsas.* You'll often see the name *mirasol* used for fresh *guajillos*. (7–8) (5)

Anaheim Probably the most popular and widely available fresh chiles in the United States, Anaheims are mild to medium hot. Most are canned, but the fresh ones are bright green, turning red as they ripen, about 6–9 inches long, and pointed. Used mainly in green chile sauces, stews, and *salsas,* they can also be stuffed for *rellenos,* or added to drinks and dressings. They are also called California, New Mexico, or Rio Grande green chiles. (3–5)

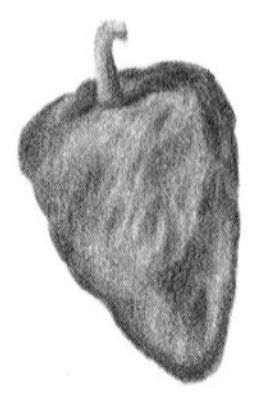

Ancho The dried version of *poblano,* these chiles are wide, heart-shaped, usually dark red to brown or black in color, and quite mild in taste. They are used in sauces, particularly Mexican *moles.* (3–5)

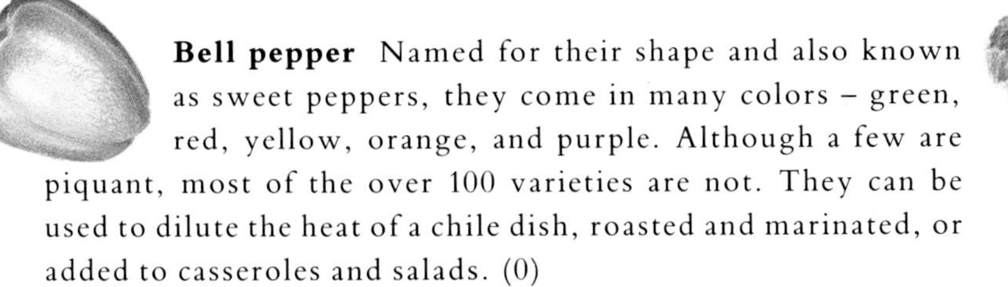

Bell pepper Named for their shape and also known as sweet peppers, they come in many colors – green, red, yellow, orange, and purple. Although a few are piquant, most of the over 100 varieties are not. They can be used to dilute the heat of a chile dish, roasted and marinated, or added to casseroles and salads. (0)

Cascabel The "little rattles" or "jingle bells" are named after the sound they make when shaken. Beautifully round and reddish-black in color, they have thick flesh with warm flavor and are excellent in stews, soups, and *salsas*. They are usually sold dried. (4)

Cayenne Bright, red, 2–3 inches long, and thin, cayennes are very hot when fresh. However, they are usually dried and ground into powder. An important ingredient in curries and Cajun dishes, cayennes are similar to *chiles de árbol*. (8)

Cherry Named for its similarity to the fruit, these chiles are scarlet, thick-fleshed, a touch sweet, and most commonly found in Hungary and other parts of Eastern Europe. Available pickled, they are good in salads or added to salsas. (1–3)

Chile de árbol Small, thin, red, and quite hot, *chiles de árbol* are similar to cayenne chiles. The name refers to the plant's resemblance to a small tree. (8)

Chipotle This dried, smoked version of red *jalapeños* has a nutty flavor and light-brown, veined skin. They are available canned in tomato-based *adobo* (or *adobado*) sauce or pickled *en escabeche,* and are especially good in soups and stews. (5–6)

Fresno Named for the first place they were grown, these small chiles are bright green, look much like *jalapeños,* and, though slightly milder in flavor, make a good substitute for them. (7)

Guajillo Also called *mirasol* when fresh, these dried brown-orange to purple-red chiles are 4–6 inches long and 1 inch wide. Among the most common chiles in Mexico, their piney, green-tea flavor is excellent in seafood. (2–4)

Habanero Named for Havana, but also called Scot Bonnet or Bahamian chiles, *habaneros* are the hottest cultivated chiles. They are lantern-shaped and come in many colors, including red, yellow, orange, and green. Used in West Indian jerk sauces and fresh *salsas,* they are sold pickled, fresh, or dried. Use with caution. (10)

Hungarian wax These yellow peppers come both sweet and hot: the sweet are long and pointy; the hot are short, conical with a smoother waxy surface. The hot peppers are frequently pickled to eat as a relish, or chopped and added to sauces. Fresh, they can be used in place of *jalapeños.* (0) (8)

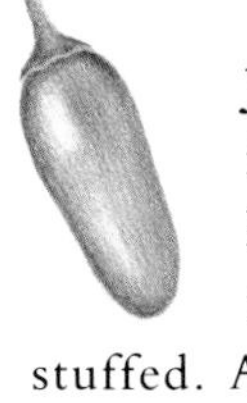

Jalapeño Available green or red (the mature fruit), fresh, canned, or pickled, these are the best-known hot chiles in the United States. Extremely versatile, they can be used in sauces, stews, *salsas* and *tamales,* or stuffed. A good substitute for any hot chile, they are recognized by their slim, slightly rounded, 2–3 inch-long shape. Dried red *jalapeños* are called *chipotles.* (8)

Lombok From Indonesia, these small, pointed, red chiles are similar to Tabasco chiles and are used in hot Indonesian dishes such as *gado gado* and *sambals.* (8)

Pasilla Also known as *chiles negros,* true pasillas are thin, 5–7 inches long, dark green when fresh, and dark brown to black when dried. When fresh, they are used for *rellenos.* They are mainly used dried or powdered and possess a licorice flavor similar to the *ancho, poblano,* or *mulato* chiles. They are excellent in seafood or *moles.* (3–5)

Pequín Also known as *chile piquín* or Birdseye, these dried red chiles are tiny and blisteringly hot. They are used for liquid hot pepper seasoning, in Thai cuisine, and to make relishes, soups, stews, and vinegars. The green fruits are generally pickled, while the ripe, red ones are dried and may be substituted for *tepíns,* and *chiles de árbol.*(7–9)

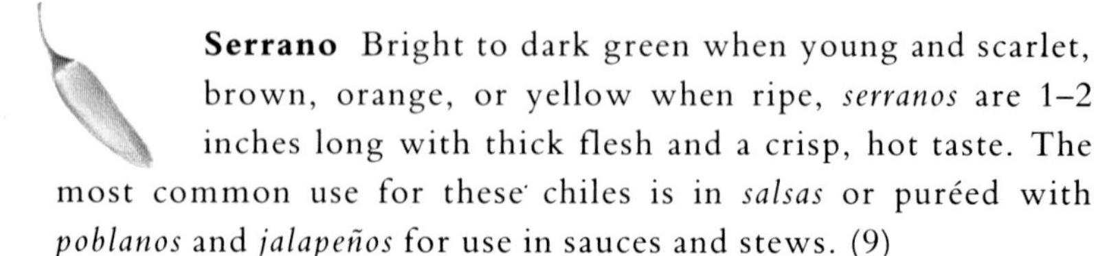

Serrano Bright to dark green when young and scarlet, brown, orange, or yellow when ripe, *serranos* are 1–2 inches long with thick flesh and a crisp, hot taste. The most common use for these chiles is in *salsas* or puréed with *poblanos* and *jalapeños* for use in sauces and stews. (9)

Tabasco Named after their Mexican region of origin, these little chiles are quite hot. Now cultivated in Louisiana, their fame has been spread by their use in liquid hot pepper seasoning. When immature, the pods are light green, then yellow, ripening to orange and red. They can be added fresh to *salsas,* cocktails, seafood dishes, and stews. (9)

Thai Green or red and very small — no longer than 1½ inches — these chiles are usually thin-fleshed with lots of seeds and a fair amount of heat. They are common in Southeast Asian cooking, in Thai curry pastes, and Thai salads. (7)

Growing Chiles

Chiles are generally easy to grow. They are annuals grown during the warmer months, but you can grow enough to last the whole year round.

Sow the seeds indoors in containers 6–8 weeks before you intend to set out plants in the garden. Keep them in a warm place (about 75°F) in full sun. Keep potting soil moist but not soaked. Set out plants one week or more after last frost date, when the temperature is at least 65°F. If the seedlings start to

get a little leggy before planting out, pinch them back, to help them grow more bushy.

Choose a sunny spot for your chiles and plant them 1–2 feet apart in well-drained soil. The plants need regular watering. Ideal temperatures are 70–85°F during the day and a slightly cooler 65°F at night. You may be able to grow the plants in containers or greenhouses, but make sure they always have plenty of sunlight.

The plants take about 2 months or more to produce fruit after planting out. The pods can be picked green, or leave them on the plant another month to mature more: depending on the variety, many may turn brown, purple, orange, or yellow; most eventually turn red or brown-black. They'll get sweeter, but not hotter.

Selecting Chiles

Fresh chiles Look for shiny chiles and sweet peppers that have a good, true color, avoiding blemished or older-looking, wrinkled ones. Mature chiles should be a good weight for their size, with a fresh, clean smell.

Dried chiles Look for good color, avoiding those that are very dry or dusty or blemished. Look for specimens with elasticity and a good earthy smell.

Chili powders Look for bright color, a sign of freshness. Avoid buying in large quantities, even if you are an avid user, because the flavor fades more quickly in the ground spice than in the whole chile.

Storing & Preserving Chiles

Drying Select chiles that have already begun to turn red. String the chiles by first tying the stems of 2 or 3 chiles together, then threading these clusters onto a longer string. Suspend in an airy place and in full sun. When using a food dehydrator, remove the seeds, cut the chiles into pieces, and let dry. Or dry on a rack in the oven (200°F) for 6–8 hours.

Pickling *Habaneros, jalapeños,* and Thai peppers are ideal for pickling. To make your own, put 1 pound chiles and 1 quart

distilled white vinegar in a pan. Bring to a boil, then set aside to cool. Store in sterilized jars in a cool, dark place.

Storing Fresh chiles can be kept in the refrigerator for up to 1 week. Store in a paper bag or wrapped in paper towels. Plastic makes the chiles sweat and spoil more quickly. Dried chiles should be stored in an airtight container in a dry, dark place. They will keep indefinitely.

Cooking with Chiles

Be cautious when handling chiles: wear rubber gloves to prevent the *capsaicin* from contacting your skin; avoid touching your eyes, nose, or other sensitive areas; wash hands and surfaces that do contact the chiles. When cooking, take care not to burn chiles – fumes can be painful, even harmful, when inhaled.

Roasting fresh chiles Preheat the oven to 400°F. Lay chiles or sweet peppers on a baking sheet and roast in the oven for about 30–35 minutes, or until the skins begin to blister. Turn them occasionally so they cook evenly. Or, roast over an open flame or directly under a hot broiler for 3–4 minutes until the skins begin to blacken and blister. When done, remove them from the oven and immediately put into a plastic bag or covered bowl. Let sit for 20 minutes or until cool, then rub off the skins. Use immediately, or marinate, covered in a good olive oil. For extra flavor, add roasted garlic, basil, and a splash of balsamic vinegar to the marinade; they will keep for up to 2 weeks, packed in sterilized jars in the refrigerator.

Using dried chiles First roast in a preheated oven (400°F) for 3–4 minutes. Don't allow them to burn. Or, drop into hot oil for 1 minute, lift out, and remove the seeds and stems. Cover with boiling water and soak for about 20 minutes. Purée the chiles with a little of the soaking water and add by the spoonful to whatever you are cooking. For more subtle spicing, sauté a dried chile in oil for 1–2 minutes, remove and discard the chile, then use the flavored oil for sautéing or marinades.

Always begin with a small amount of chile, adding more as needed. For mouth burns, eat starchy foods, such as rice or bread, sweets, yogurt, lemons, or limes, or drink beer. Water merely prolongs the pain.

Chili Sherry

25-ounce bottle (or 3 cups) fino *sherry*
3 whole cloves
5–7 fresh Anaheim *chiles, roasted, seeded, and halved*
1 vanilla pod

Put all the ingredients into a bottle; let sit for at least 1 month. The flavor will improve with age.

This is excellent used in cooking, particularly in stir-fried dishes. It is also reputed to improve coughs and colds, taken a spoonful at a time. *Makes about 3 cups.*

Chili Oil

2½ cups peanut or vegetable oil
12 fresh red Thai chiles

Heat the oil in a heavy-bottomed skillet over medium heat. When the oil is sizzling, remove from the heat and carefully add the chiles. Let stand for at least 24 hours, then transfer to a bottle and store in the refrigerator for a few weeks. This oil is wonderful for barbecuing and stir-frying, and for pepping up stews and soups. *Makes about 2½ cups.*

Hot Guajillo Pesto

2 large heads garlic

2 dried guajillo *chiles, roasted, seeded, and soaked*

⅔ cup chopped fresh basil

1 cup freshly grated Parmesan cheese

2 cups toasted pine nuts

3 tablespoons olive oil

Preheat the oven to 375°F. Cut off the top one-quarter of the garlic heads, brush with oil, wrap in foil, and place in the oven for 45–60 minutes. Cool, then press out the softened garlic.

Purée the garlic with the other ingredients in a food processor, adding the olive oil gradually, until smooth. Store, airtight, in the refrigerator; use to marinate meat and seafood, or add to pastas, soups, and stews. *Makes about 4 cups.*

Spicy Tomato Chutney

4 pounds ripe tomatoes, coarsely chopped
1 pound onions, thinly sliced
2 tablespoons salt and 1 tablespoon coarsely ground black pepper
3 chipotle *chiles, roasted and seeded*
2 teaspoons Dijon mustard
1 rounded tablespoon Indian Curry Powder (page 23)
½ cup red wine vinegar
1 cup superfine sugar

Put the tomatoes and onions in a large bowl and sprinkle with the salt. Cover and allow to stand overnight. (The salt extracts the liquid from the tomatoes and onions.)

Pour the liquid away, then rinse the tomatoes and onions under cold running water. Put into a strainer and press out any remaining liquid.

Soak the chiles in boiling water for 20 minutes. Strain, retaining 2 tablespoons of the water. Place the chiles in a blender or food processor. Add 1 tablespoon of the chile soaking water and purée. If necessary, add the remaining 1 tablespoon soaking water to obtain a purée. Set aside.

Place the onions and tomatoes in a saucepan and cook over medium heat for 10 minutes, then crush the tomatoes with the back of a spoon. Add the mustard, curry powder, and puréed chiles. Reduce the heat to low and simmer for about 15 minutes.

Meanwhile, bring the vinegar and sugar to a boil and cook until reduced by two-thirds. Add this to the tomato mixture with the black pepper and stir well. As the chutney thickens, stir often to prevent sticking. Simmer for 30 minutes more, or until thickened. Taste for seasoning and spiciness. While still hot, pour into sterilized jars and seal immediately. Keep unopened in a cool place for 3 months. *Makes about 1½ pounds.*

Mexican Chili Paste

8 dried Pasilla *chiles, roasted, seeded, and soaked*
2 dried ancho *chiles, roasted, seeded, and soaked*
2 dried cascabel *chiles, roasted, seeded, and soaked*
2 dried chipotle *chiles, roasted, seeded, and soaked*
1 dried cayenne or Tabasco *chile, roasted, seeded, and soaked*
1 medium onion, sliced
2 cloves garlic, sliced
½ teaspoon cumin seeds
1½ teaspoons coriander seeds
¼ teaspoon fennel seeds
½ teaspoon ground cinnamon
½ teaspoon salt
1½ teaspoons roasted almonds
2 tablespoons sesame seeds, toasted
2 tablespoons raisins
1 large tomato, peeled
½ slice stale white bread, cubed

Place all the chiles, onions, and garlic in a blender or food processor and process until smooth. Slowly add the remaining spices, nuts, seeds, raisins, tomato, and enough bread to make a thick paste. You may have to blend the ingredients in batches and add a little water if too thick. This paste is delicious in stews and casseroles. Keep covered in the refrigerator for 2–4 weeks. *Makes about 2½ cups.*

Indian Curry Powder

6 fresh cayenne chiles, seeded
1 tablespoon coriander seeds
1 tablespoon cumin seeds
1 tablespoon mustard seeds
1 tablespoon chopped fresh ginger
2 teaspoons black peppercorns
2 teaspoons turmeric
8 curry leaves, torn

Heat a heavy-bottomed skillet and, in separate batches, dry roast first the chiles, then the coriander, cumin, mustard seeds, and finally the ginger, for about 1 minute each. Cool and grind into a powder with the peppercorns, turmeric, and curry leaves.

This will keep for about 2 months in an airtight container. Add this curry powder to Indian dishes; it can also be used in dips or marinades. *Makes about 1/2–2/3 cup.*

NOTE Curry leaves are available at Asian markets. Making your own curry powder can be extremely therapeutic. It also lends a distinctive flavor to curries that cannot be bought!

Green Thai Chili Paste

1 small onion
3 cloves garlic
2 stalks lemongrass, cut into strips
1 tablespoon coriander seeds
1 teaspoon cumin seeds
1 teaspoon black peppercorns
4–6 green Thai chiles (seeded, if desired, for milder taste)
2 tablespoons chopped fresh cilantro
1 tablespoon finely chopped galangal or ginger
Grated zest of 2 limes
2 teaspoons trassi *(dried shrimp paste, also known as* blanchan*)*
1 tablespoon raw sugar

Roughly chop the onion, garlic, and lemongrass. In a heavy-bottomed skillet, combine the coriander seeds, cumin seeds, and peppercorns, and dry roast over medium-high heat for 2–3 minutes, until they begin to darken. Cool and grind into a powder. Put the whole chiles and the remaining ingredients in a food processor and purée, scraping down the sides of processor bowl frequently, until it forms a rich, green paste (4–5 minutes). The

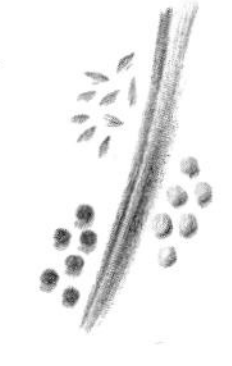

paste can be kept in an airtight container in the refrigerator for up to 1 week. *Makes about ¾ cup.*

NOTE For Red Thai Chili Paste, substitute red chiles for the green chiles and omit the cilantro. These pastes will lend a Southeast Asian flavor to any dish and are especially good in curries. They should be dry fried in the wok first before the other ingredients are added.

Satay Sauce

1 tablespoon peanut oil
3 tablespoons Red Thai Chili Paste (page 25)
1 cup coconut milk
1 tablespoon soy sauce
2 teaspoons lime juice
2 teaspoons raw sugar
1 tablespoon roasted slivered almonds
1¾–2 cups peanuts, crushed

In a heavy-bottomed skillet, over medium heat, warm the oil, add the Red Thai Chili Paste, and stir for 3 minutes. Add the coconut milk. Bring to a boil, stirring constantly, then add the remaining ingredients. Reduce heat to low and simmer, uncovered, for 5 minutes more.

The sauce should be fairly thick but may be diluted with a little water, if needed. It will keep in the refrigerator for 2–3 days. *Makes about 2 cups.*

NOTE This is an excellent dip or sauce, served with all types of broiled or barbecued meats, fish, or vegetables.

Sweet Pepper Vinaigrette

2 pounds mixed red and yellow bell peppers
1 cup olive oil
½ cup sweet white wine
½ cup white wine vinegar
1 tablespoon raw sugar
3 tablespoons chopped fresh parsley
1 teaspoon each salt and freshly ground black pepper

In a large pan over medium heat, toss the peppers in half the oil, until you can smell their aroma. Add the wine, vinegar, and sugar, bring to a boil, then reduce the heat to low. Cover and simmer gently, checking occasionally that the peppers are not sticking. After 1 hour, spoon the contents of the pan into a food processor or blender and purée, adding the remaining oil and the fresh parsley. Add the seasoning, and serve warm or at room temperature. This is excellent with terrines and shellfish. *Makes about 2 cups.*

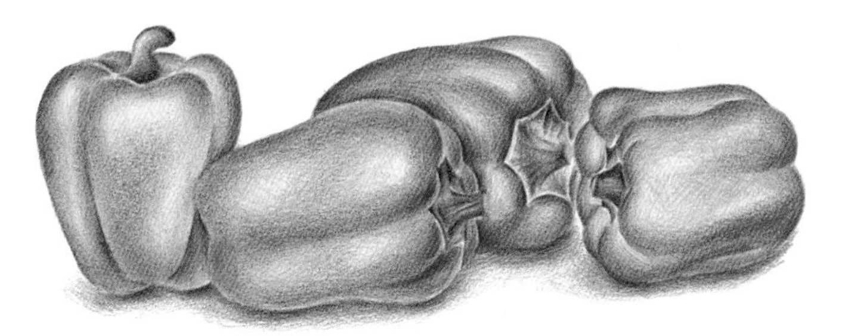

Mango Salsa

2–3 serrano *chiles, seeded and finely chopped*
¾ pound peeled and diced mango
1 small red onion, coarsely chopped
1 tablespoon chopped fresh cilantro
2 teaspoons chopped fresh ginger
1 tablespoon olive oil

Combine all the ingredients and leave in the refrigerator for at least 1 hour, so that the flavors can blend. This dish is best eaten within a few hours, and is excellent served with fish. *Makes about 1½ cups.*

Tomato & Black Olive Salsa

¾ pound Roma tomatoes

3 chipotle *chiles, soaked and chopped, or 2* jalapeño *chiles, roasted, seeded, and finely diced*

1 small red onion, finely chopped

1 cup kalamata olives, pitted and chopped

1 tablespoon extra-virgin olive oil

2 teaspoons red or white wine vinegar

1 teaspoon dry sherry

1 teaspoon each salt and freshly ground black pepper

Chop the tomatoes into small cubes. Place in a bowl with either the dried or the fresh chiles, onion, olives, oil, vinegar, sherry, and seasoning. Chill for up to 2 hours to allow the flavors to blend. *Makes about 2 cups.*

NOTE This salsa can be served with red meats or with broiled fish, such as swordfish or tuna steaks.

Spicy Tomato Soup

¾ cup Spicy Tomato Chutney (page 20)
4¼ cups tomato juice
⅓ cup mixed fresh herbs, such as parsley, basil, and mint
½ teaspoon salt and 1 teaspoon coarse black pepper
5–6 tablespoons yogurt
2 tablespoons chopped fresh mint

In a saucepan, combine the Spicy Tomato Chutney and the tomato juice, and bring to a boil over high heat. Reduce heat to low after 5 minutes, then add the herbs and seasoning and continue to simmer for 5 minutes more.

Ladle into soup plates and serve with a swirl of yogurt and a sprinkling of mint. *Makes about 5 cups.*

Lah-lah Soup (Pacific Fish Soup)

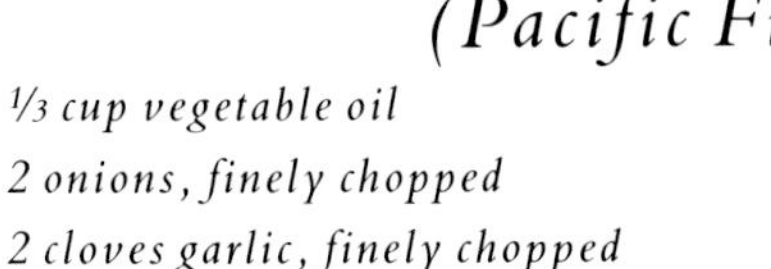

1/3 cup vegetable oil
2 onions, finely chopped
2 cloves garlic, finely chopped
3 tablespoons chopped fresh ginger
1 tablespoon turmeric
1/2 pound mixed fish fillets, cubed
2 1/2 cups chicken broth
Juice of 3 limes
6 fresh red Thai chiles, seeded and finely chopped
3 tablespoons fish sauce
2 stalks lemongrass
3 tablespoons sugar
2 1/2 cups coconut cream
1 cup chopped fresh cilantro

In a medium-size pan, heat the oil, the onions, garlic, and ginger and stir continuously for 1 minute. Add the turmeric and combine well. Add the fish and cook for 2 minutes more. Add the remaining ingredients, except the coconut cream and chopped cilantro. Reduce the heat to low and simmer gently until the fish is opaque throughout. Stir in the coconut cream and cilantro, simmer for 2 minutes more, until heated through, and serve hot. *Serves 4.*

Sevillian Roast Pepper Gazpacho

2 pounds ripe tomatoes, cored
3 tablespoons olive oil
3 red bell peppers and 2 yellow bell peppers, roasted, peeled, and seeded
2 slices white bread, crusts removed
2 small Bermuda or red onions, coarsely chopped
3 cloves garlic, coarsely chopped
1¼ cups tomato juice
1 tablespoon red wine vinegar
1 teaspoon dry sherry
1 cucumber, peeled and coarsely chopped
Large pinch cayenne pepper
2 teaspoons each salt and freshly ground black pepper

Garnishes

4–6 tablespoons whipping cream or yogurt
⅓ cup croûtons
⅓ cup chopped green bell peppers
⅓ cup pitted and chopped ripe olives
1 tablespoon chopped fresh basil

Preheat the oven to 475°F. Place the tomatoes on a baking sheet, brush with the olive oil, and roast in the oven for 15 minutes. Cool tomatoes and peel.

Pour the juice from the roasted tomatoes into a blender or food processor, then add the tomatoes, peppers, bread, onions, and garlic (you may need to process the ingredients in batches). Pulse in 5 second bursts, until the mixture is a rough pulp. Add the remaining gazpacho ingredients and continue to purée in short bursts until just blended. Chill for 4–6 hours. Thin with a little chilled water, if necessary. Serve cold with a swirl of cream or yogurt and the selection of garnishes. *Serves 4.*

NOTE Recipes for gazpacho are merely beginnings. This one is a good start but there are many other ingredients that could be added, such as chopped scallions, diced avocado, tiny cooked shrimp, chopped cilantro, or chopped pickled *jalapeños*. Experiment!

Jumbo Shrimp with Thai Dipping Sauce

1 tablespoon Green Thai Chili Paste (page 24)
Juice of 4 limes
3 tablespoons chopped fresh ginger
1 pound jumbo shrimp, peeled and deveined
¼ cup peanut oil

Dipping sauce

2 carrots, finely diced
½ medium cucumber, finely diced
2 red Thai chiles, seeded and finely chopped
4 shallots, minced
1 clove garlic, minced
1 cup white wine vinegar
¾ cup raw sugar
3 tablespoons water
1 teaspoon chopped fresh cilantro

In a ceramic or glass bowl, mix the Green Thai Chili Paste, lime juice, and ginger. Add the shrimp and marinate for 1 hour.

Meanwhile, to make the dipping sauce, place the finely diced carrot, cucumber, chiles, shallots, and garlic in a bowl and set aside. Bring the vinegar and sugar to a boil in a small pan over high heat until the liquid is reduced by about one-third, about

10 minutes. (Special care must be taken not to reduce the liquid too much, as the sugar hardens. If this happens, mix in some warm water to dilute. The best consistency is a runny syrup.) While still hot, pour the sauce over the vegetables, stir in the cilantro, and let cool.

Heat the peanut oil in a wok over high heat, add the shrimp, and cook for 2-3 minutes, or until they turn pink and are slightly crisp. With a slotted spoon, transfer the shrimp to a platter. Serve with the dipping sauce on the side. *Serves 4.*

NOTE Sauce also good with broiled fish or chicken.

Curry & Cilantro Mussels

1 large onion, finely chopped
3 cloves garlic, crushed
1 tablespoon chopped fresh ginger
⅓ cup Indian Curry Powder (page 23)
⅓ cup ghee or clarified butter
½ cup dry white wine
2 pequín chiles, seeded and chopped
2 pounds mussels
¼ cup whipping cream
⅓ cup chopped fresh cilantro

Combine the onion, garlic, ginger, and curry powder in a food processor or blender. Add the ghee and blend until it forms a paste. Place a large saucepan over medium heat, add the curry paste, and stir vigorously to prevent sticking. Add the wine and chiles, reduce the heat to low, and simmer, covered, for 2–3 minutes. Scrub and beard the mussels, and add to the pan. Cover and continue to simmer for about 5 minutes, or until the shells open. Add the cream and stir gently, making sure all the mussels are coated with the juices. Cook for 2 minutes more. Discard any unopened mussels, stir in the cilantro, and serve piping hot. *Serves 4.*

NOTE Try serving these mussels in the Belgian manner, with *pommes frites* — French fries. Delicious!

Roasted Bell Pepper Sorbet with Vodka

2 red bell peppers, roasted, peeled, and seeded
1 stalk celery, chopped
4 tablespoons Spicy Tomato Chutney (page 20)
6 tablespoons tomato juice
4 tablespoons vodka
Juice of 1 lemon
1 teaspoon celery salt
4 teaspoons liquid hot pepper seasoning or 2 Tabasco *chiles, seeded and finely chopped*
1 teaspoon coarsely ground black pepper
Few stalks celery, with leaves
Few lemon slices

Place the sweet peppers, celery, chutney, and tomato juice in a blender or food processor and whirl to a slightly coarse texture. Add the vodka, lemon juice, celery salt, liquid hot pepper seasoning, and pepper. Whirl again until smoothly puréed. Place in the freezer until the sorbet begins to freeze, about 2 hours, then purée again. Refreeze for 8 hours, then purée the sorbet once more. Cover and store in freezer. Let soften at room temperature about 10 minutes before serving. Serve in a glass with a celery stalk and a twist of lemon. *Serves 4.*

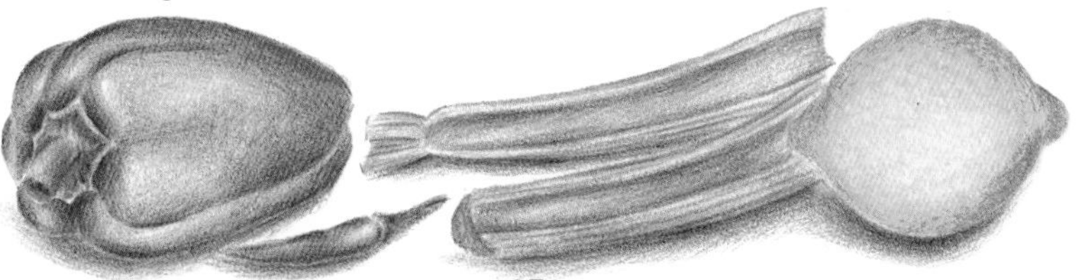

Sambal Bajak (Peanut & Chile Fruit Salad)

5 cloves garlic
1 tablespoon olive oil
4 dried red Lombok *chiles, or any hot red variety, seeded and chopped*
8 shallots, finely chopped
1 teaspoon trassi *(dried shrimp paste, also known as* blanchan*)*
¼ cup chopped roasted cashews or peanuts
3 tablespoons vegetable oil
1 teaspoon brown sugar
2 teaspoons chopped fresh cilantro
½ teaspoon salt
½ cup thick coconut cream
2 unripe mangoes, peeled and cubed
2 unripe papayas, peeled and cubed
1 star fruit, sliced crosswise
3 pineapple rings

To roast the garlic, preheat the oven to 375°F. Cut off the top one-quarter of the heads, brush with the oil, wrap tightly in foil, and place in the oven for 30–45 minutes. Cool, then press out the softened garlic. Combine the chiles, shallots, *trassi*, roasted garlic, and nuts in a food processor and whirl until puréed. Heat the oil in a skillet, add the chili paste, and sauté over medium heat for 1–2 minutes. Stir in the sugar, cilantro, salt, and coconut cream. Reduce the heat to low and simmer gently for 15 minutes more, until the *sambal* thickens into a wet paste. Place the fruit in a serving bowl. Mix the *sambal* into the fruit or serve on the side as a relish. *Sambal* can be stored in the refrigerator for up to 1 week and served hot or cold. *Serves 4.*

NOTE *Sambal*, a relish from Indonesia, can be made as hot or mild as you like, by adding more or less chiles. Here the sweet, hot *sambal* is added to a mixture of sour fruits to make an unusual appetizer or side dish.

Crispy Peking Duck Salad

Marinade

Juice of 1 orange
1 tablespoon honey
6 fresh red chiles, seeded and finely chopped
1 cup soy sauce
¼ cup dry sherry
2 scallions, finely chopped
¼ cup coarsely chopped fresh ginger

Vinaigrette

1½ teaspoons orange juice
1 tablespoon wine vinegar
3 tablespoons vegetable oil
1½ teaspoons sesame oil

¾ pound boneless duck breast
4 cups torn mixed lettuce leaves
1 bunch watercress, trimmed
1 orange, sliced in rounds
8 tablespoons toasted, slivered almonds

To make the marinade, combine the orange juice and honey in a saucepan over medium-high heat, stirring until the honey has melted. Add the remaining marinade ingredients and combine well. Put the duck in a heatproof dish. Add the marinade, cover, and refrigerate for 24 hours.

To make the vinaigrette, combine the orange juice and vinegar in a small bowl. Whisk in the oils. Set aside.

Preheat the oven to 325°F. Place the duck on a rack in a broiler pan and cook for 1 hour. Then broil 4–6 inches below heat until the duck begins to blacken, turn over and repeat on the other side. The duck is done when both sides are slightly blackened.

Place lettuce in a large bowl, add some of the vinaigrette, and toss until evenly coated. Transfer salad to a platter. Cut the duck into thin, slanting slices and fan out on top of the lettuce. Drizzle with some of the pan juices, then the remaining vinaigrette. Arrange the watercress and orange slices around the platter and sprinkle with the almonds. *Serves 4.*

Seviche Mauritius

1 pound white fish fillets, frozen then thawed in the refrigerator
1 cup lime juice
2 dried guajillo *chiles, roasted, seeded, and soaked*
1 medium onion, cut into rings
1 clove garlic, minced
¼ teaspoon each salt and freshly ground black pepper
1 mango, peeled and cubed
1 pineapple, cut into rings
4–6 lime wedges
Several sprigs cilantro

Slice the fish fillets into thin, finger-size strips. Put in a glass or ceramic dish and cover with the lime juice, chiles, onion, garlic, and seasoning. Cover and refrigerate for 12 hours.

In a heavy-bottomed skillet, cook the mango and pineapple over high heat, stirring constantly, for 1 minute, or just until warmed. Serve the warmed fruit with the fish. Garnish with lime wedges and sprigs of cilantro. *Serves 4.*

Smoked Turkey with Hot Quince Sauce

1 tablespoon fruit vinegar
1 tablespoon red wine vinegar
½ teaspoon salt and 1 teaspoon freshly ground black pepper
3 tablespoons olive oil
4–6 cups torn mixed lettuce leaves
¾ pound smoked turkey or chicken, thickly sliced
Few chervil sprigs

Sauce
¼ cup quince jelly
⅔ cup red wine
1 whole cayenne chile, seeded and finely chopped
1 teaspoon coarsely ground black pepper
1 tablespoon brown sugar (optional)

In a small bowl, combine the vinegars and salt. Gradually whisk in the oil until blended. Add the pepper and set aside.

To make the sauce, combine the jelly and wine in a large saucepan over moderate heat and stir until the jelly begins to dissolve. Add the chile and black pepper and stir for 2 minutes. Add the sugar, if desired. Strain the sauce, then return it to the saucepan. Simmer for 2–3 minutes, or until thick.

Toss the lettuce leaves with 2–3 tablespoons of the vinaigrette, then divide among 4 plates. Add the meat to the sauce just to warm through. With a slotted spoon, transfer the meat to the beds of lettuce. Spoon the sauce over each, garnish with the chervil, and serve immediately. *Serves 4.*

Polenta with Habanero Chiles & Cheese

4¼ cups water
2 teaspoons salt
1 cup quick-cooking polenta
2 tablespoons unsalted butter
2 egg yolks
1 habanero *chile, seeded and minced*
1 teaspoon paprika
¾ cup freshly grated Parmesan cheese

Preheat the oven to 400°F. Bring the water and salt to a boil in a large heavy-bottomed saucepan. When the water boils, add the polenta in a thin stream, stirring continuously. Stir and cook for 4 minutes, then remove from the heat. Stir in the butter, egg yolks, chile, paprika, and two-thirds of the cheese. The polenta should now be thick but pourable.

Pour the mixture into a greased 9-inch square cake pan, sprinkle with the remaining cheese, and bake for 20 minutes, or until the polenta is firm. Serve hot or cold. *Serves 4.*

NOTE As an alternative, cut the cooked and cooled polenta into ½-inch thick slices and broil until beginning to brown. This offers a pleasant change from potatoes, rice, or cornbread.

Blackened Cajun Fish Fillets

½ teaspoon cumin seeds
1 clove garlic, coarsely chopped
½ small onion, coarsely chopped
½ teaspoon dry mustard
2 teaspoon paprika
1 tablespoon cayenne pepper
1 teaspoon dried thyme
1 teaspoon dried oregano
1 teaspoon each salt and lemon pepper seasoning
1 teaspoon mace
2 teaspoons chopped pimento peppers
4 red snapper, sole, or perch fillets

Heat a heavy-bottomed skillet over high heat, add the cumin seeds, and dry roast for 2–3 minutes, or until they darken. Place in a food processor with all the ingredients but the fish and whirl into a smooth paste. Cover the fish with the paste. Place the fish in a heavy-bottomed skillet and cook over high heat for about 5 minutes, or until cooked through and blackened. Serve with sweet potatoes and a salad. *Serves 4.*

NOTE This seasoning base is used in many Cajun dishes and can be used in stews, gumbos, or for blackening poultry and meats under a broiler or on the barbecue.

Sotong Sambal (Baby Squid Stuffed with Sweet Potato)

16 baby squid
3 fresh red Lombok *chiles, or other hot red variety, seeded and finely chopped*
3 tablespoons Red Thai Chili Paste (page 25)
Grated zest and juice of 4 limes
⅔ cup soy sauce
4–5 tablespoons fresh ginger, cut into thin strips
3 tablespoons sweet sherry
2 medium sweet potatoes, peeled and quartered
4 shallots, finely chopped
2 tablespoons sesame oil
3 tablespoons chopped fresh cilantro
1 teaspoon ground cumin
2 tablespoons butter or margarine
2 tablespoons vegetable oil

Remove the spine and insides of the squid. Separate the tentacles from the body and wash both well. Combine the chiles, Red Thai Chili Paste, grated lime zest, soy sauce, ginger, and sherry in a shallow dish. Add the squid and toss until well coated. Cover and marinate in the refrigerator for 6 hours.

Put the sweet potatoes in a saucepan and add cold water to cover. Bring to a boil, then reduce the heat and simmer for 20 minutes, or until soft. Drain; keep warm.

In a small skillet, sauté the shallots in sesame oil over

medium-high heat until they begin to color; add the cilantro, cumin, and the lime juice. Add to the sweet potatoes and mash until smooth. Spoon the mixture into a pastry bag and carefully pipe into each squid body. Use a toothpick to enclose the stuffing and attach the tentacles. Heat butter and oil in a wide skillet over high heat. Add squid and cook, turning once, until browned on each side. The squid should be watched carefully as overcooking can make them rubbery. Add half the marinade. The squid are done when the liquid comes to a boil. *Serves 4.*

Red-hot Red Snapper

4 red snapper fillets (about 8 ounces each)
3 fresh jalapeño *chiles, seeded and finely chopped*
2 medium onions, finely sliced
2 cloves garlic, finely chopped
1 tablespoon chopped fresh ginger
1 teaspoon Indian Curry Powder (page 23)
1 teaspoon cumin seeds
1 teaspoon salt
1 teaspoon chopped fresh cilantro
1 tablespoon lemon juice
2 kiwi fruits, peeled and sliced
½ cup yogurt or fromage frais
2–3 tablespoons vegetable oil

Garnishes

1 fresh mango, peeled, pitted, and sliced
4-inch piece ginger, peeled and grated

Lay the fish in a shallow glass or ceramic dish. In a bowl, combine the remaining ingredients, except the oil, adding the yogurt last and mixing just until blended. Pour over the fillets, cover, and marinate in the refrigerator for 24 hours.

Divide the mango slices among 4 plates. Sprinkle with the grated ginger and set aside. Preheat the broiler. Remove the fish, reserving the marinade. Blot the fish dry, brush with the oil, and broil on both sides for 2–3 minutes, until the fish is opaque and beginning to brown at the edges. Slowly heat the marinade, stirring for 2 minutes. Put 1 fish fillet on each plate, next to the mango slices. Drizzle the sauce over the fish. *Serves 4.*

Penne, Peppers & Parmesan

3 cloves garlic, crushed or minced
½ cup olive oil
1 pound mixed green, yellow, and red bell peppers, roasted, peeled, seeded, and thinly sliced
½ pound spinach, blanched, squeezed dry, and chopped
⅓ cup toasted pine nuts
½ cup sun-dried tomatoes packed in oil, coarsely chopped
½ teaspoon salt and 2 teaspoons freshly ground black pepper
1 pound penne *pasta*
1 cup freshly grated Parmesan cheese
Few basil sprigs

In a large skillet, sauté the garlic in olive oil over medium heat for 2–3 minutes, or until it begins to brown. Add the peppers, spinach, pine nuts, sun-dried tomatoes, and seasoning and cook for 3–4 minutes, or until heated through. Remove from the heat.

Bring a large pot of salted water to a boil. Add the pasta and cook just until tender to the bite. Drain the pasta, then return to the pan. Add the sauce and Parmesan. Garnish with the basil. *Serves 4.*

Provençal Vegetable Tart

Pastry

1½ cups all-purpose flour
½ cup butter
¼ teaspoon cayenne
1 egg, beaten

1 small eggplant (about ¼ pound), thinly sliced
4 tablespoons olive oil
1 medium zucchini (about ¼ pound), thinly sliced
1 large leek, trimmed and sliced
2–3 cloves garlic, crushed or minced
2 medium tomatoes (about ½ pound), peeled, seeded, and chopped
1 red bell pepper, roasted, seeded, and cut into strips
2 tablespoons chopped fresh basil
2 eggs
⅔ cup milk
½ teaspoon salt

To make the pastry, combine the flour and butter in a food processor, using on-off pulses until coarse crumbs form. Add the cayenne and egg and whirl until the mixture forms a ball. Wrap in waxed paper and refrigerate for at least 30 minutes.

Meanwhile, preheat the oven to 375°F. Place the eggplant on a baking sheet, brush on both sides with 2 tablespoons of the oil, and bake for 25–30 minutes until tender. Heat the remaining oil in a large skillet over medium heat. Add the zucchini, leek, and garlic, and cook for about 5 minutes until softened. Set aside.

Press the dough evenly over the bottom and sides of a 9-inch tart pan. Prick all over with a fork, line with foil, and fill with pie weights. Bake for 12 minutes. Remove foil and weights and bake for 5 minutes more.

Arrange the eggplant slices in the bottom of the pastry crust. Spoon the leek mixture on top in an even layer. Repeat with the tomatoes. Top with the red bell pepper strips. Sprinkle with the basil.

Combine the eggs, milk, and salt in a bowl and whisk until blended. Spoon the mixture over the vegetables a little at a time, waiting for each addition to settle before adding more. Bake for about 30 minutes until set. Serve hot or cold. *Serves 6.*

White Chili

2 tablespoons olive oil

2 medium onions, coarsely chopped

1 large green bell pepper, coarsely chopped

4 cloves garlic, crushed or minced

4–6 tablespoons Mexican Chili Paste (page 22)

2 pounds diced chicken or turkey

1 tablespoon dried oregano

1 tablespoon salt and 1 teaspoon white pepper

3 tablespoons tomato paste

2 pounds tomatoes, cored, peeled, seeded, and chopped

2 cups dried white beans, soaked overnight and cooked

½ cup dry white wine

1¼ cups chicken broth

1 bay leaf

Garnishes

½ cup chopped fresh cilantro

1 cup sour cream

1–2 cups shredded jalapeño Monterey Jack or Cheddar cheese

1 large onion, finely chopped

⅔ cup diced avocado

⅔ cup diced bell pepper

12 flour tortillas

In a large casserole, combine the oil, onions, and bell pepper. Cook over medium heat for about 5 minutes, until softened. Stir in the garlic and 2–3 tablespoons of the chili paste and cook for 1 minute more. Add the meat and cook for about 5 minutes, stirring, until browned. Stir in the remaining chili ingredients. Cover and simmer gently for 20 minutes.

Meanwhile, prepare the garnishes: place the cilantro, sour cream, cheese, onion, avocado, and bell pepper in separate serving bowls. Wrap the tortillas in aluminum foil and warm in a 200°F oven. Wrap in a clean napkin to keep warm.

Remove the bay leaf before serving the chili. If more spiciness is desired, add the remaining chili paste. Serve hot with the garnishes. *Serves 6.*

Laksa Jahore (Sweet Malaysian Fish Curry)

3 cups coconut milk
1 onion, chopped
16–20 shelled small shrimp (about ½ pound), deveined
1 pound fish fillets
⅓ cup unsweetened shredded coconut, toasted
3 stalks lemongrass, chopped and pounded
3 tablespoons minced galangal or ⅓ cup peeled minced fresh ginger
1 tablespoon trassi *(dried shrimp paste, also known as* blanchan*)*
1 tablespoon Green Thai Chili Paste (page 24)
3–4 fresh red Thai chiles, seeded and chopped
1 cup fish or vegetable broth
¼ cup chopped fresh mint
1 tablespoon shredded tamarind
1 tablespoon sugar
½ teaspoon salt and 1 teaspoon freshly ground black pepper
3 tablespoons sesame oil
1 pound vermicelli *or* spaghettini *pasta, cooked and drained*
½ cup coconut cream
¼ cup chopped fresh cilantro leaves

Garnishes

Chopped red onions, fresh chile slices, fried tofu slices, chopped cucumber, and Thai fish balls, if available

In a large saucepan, bring the coconut milk, onion, half the shrimp, and half the fish fillets to a boil. Reduce the heat to low and simmer for 15 minutes. Purée in a blender or food processor, then return to the heat. Pound the toasted coconut until it appears oily, then add to the pan with the lemongrass, galangal, shrimp paste, chili paste, chiles, and fish broth. Bring back to a boil, then reduce the heat to low and simmer for 15 minutes. Stir in the mint, tamarind, sugar, salt, and pepper.

Meanwhile, in a heavy-bottomed skillet, heat the sesame oil until it begins to smoke. Add the remaining fish and shrimp, and sauté quickly, but don't cook through.

Add the noodles, fried fish, and shrimp to the saucepan. Stir in the coconut cream, warm through, and sprinkle with chopped cilantro. Serve the garnishes in separate bowls on the side. *Serves 4.*

NOTE Ingredients for Malaysian cooking may be found at Indian, Asian, or Middle Eastern markets.

Catalan Chicken with Apple & Pepper Sauce

1 lemon, peeled and sliced
½ cup unsweetened apple juice
½ cup dry white wine
Leaves of 2 thyme sprigs
4 chicken breast halves (about 8 ounces each)
½ teaspoon each salt and freshly ground black pepper
¼ cup olive oil
1 pound potatoes, boiled, cubed, and sautéed

Sauce

¼ cup olive oil
2 onions, finely chopped
1 clove garlic, finely chopped
1 tablespoon chopped fresh thyme
2 sweet apples, cored and sliced
1 tablespoon tomato paste
1 pound ripe tomatoes, peeled, seeded, and chopped
⅔ cup pimento or red bell pepper, coarsely chopped
½ cup unsweetened apple juice
½ cup dry white wine
¼ teaspoon each salt and freshly ground black pepper

Combine the lemon slices, apple juice, wine, and thyme in a dish just large enough to hold the chicken. Add the chicken, turn to coat, cover, and marinate in the refrigerator for 6–8 hours.

To make the sauce, heat the oil in a medium skillet over low heat and add the chopped onions, garlic, and thyme. Cook for about 5 minutes, or until softened. Add the apples, stir for 2 minutes, then add the tomato paste and fresh tomatoes. Simmer for 2 minutes, then stir in the pimento, apple juice, wine and seasoning. Cover, and simmer gently for 30 minutes.

Remove the chicken from the marinade and pat dry; reserve the marinade. Season the chicken breasts. In a large heavy-bottomed skillet, heat the oil over high heat, add the chicken, and cook for 5 minutes, or until golden brown on both sides. Transfer the chicken breasts to a clay pot or a heavy casserole.

Preheat the oven to 350°F. Pour the reserved marinade into the skillet and boil over high heat until reduced to about one-third of the original volume. Pour the reduced marinade over the chicken, then add the potatoes and the sauce.
Bake, covered, in the oven for 25–30 minutes.
Serves 4.

Soufflé-stuffed Sweet Peppers

4 red bell peppers
4 tablespoons unsalted butter
2 cloves garlic, crushed or minced
⅓ cup milk
1 cup shredded sharp Cheddar cheese
⅓ cup freshly grated Parmesan cheese
3 large eggs, separated
2 teaspoons nutmeg
3 teaspoons chopped fresh rosemary
1 teaspoon salt and 2 teaspoons freshly ground black pepper
2 tablespoons olive oil

Preheat the oven to 375°F. Slice the tops off the peppers, then scoop out the seeds and ribs. Finely chop the tops of the peppers and set aside.

In a skillet, melt the butter over low heat, add the garlic, and sauté for 5–6 minutes, or until it begins to brown. Add the finely chopped pepper and the milk. Warm gently for about 5 minutes, then stir in half the cheese, the egg yolks, nutmeg, rosemary, salt, and pepper. Cook until the cheese melts and the mixture begins to thicken, 6–8 minutes. Remove from

the heat. Beat the egg whites until they hold stiff peaks, then fold gently into the cheese mixture.

Brush the outside of each pepper with olive oil, place on a greased baking sheet, and fill each with the soufflé mixture. Sprinkle with the remaining cheese and bake for 20–25 minutes, or until the soufflés rise above the top of the peppers. *Serves 4.*

NOTE This dish is particularly good accompanied by roasted potatoes and spinach.

Thai Beef Stir-fry

1 pound fillet steak
1 tablespoon soy sauce
1 tablespoon honey
1 tablespoon sweet sherry
4 red or green Thai chiles, seeded and chopped, or 1 tablespoon Green or Red Thai Chili Paste (page 24)
1 teaspoon sesame oil
1 Bermuda or red onion, chopped
2 cloves garlic, crushed or minced
⅓ cup peeled, chopped ginger
¼ head savoy cabbage, coarsely chopped
8 baby corn cobs, sliced into ½-inch pieces
⅔ cup trimmed green beans
2 carrots, cut into matchsticks
1 bunch watercress, stems trimmed
3–4 cups jasmine rice, steamed

Slice the steak into finger-size strips. In a bowl, mix the soy sauce, honey, sherry, and Thai Chili Paste. Add the steak, toss, and let marinate in the soy sauce mixture for up to 6 hours.

Pour the sesame oil into a wok over high heat. When the oil begins to smoke, add the onion, garlic, and ginger. Lift the beef from the marinade with a slotted spoon and add to the wok. Toss quickly to brown, about 2 minutes, then add the remaining vegetables except the watercress, stirring constantly. After 2 minutes stir in the marinade, cover, remove from the heat, and steam for 2 minutes. Add the watercress, stir once or twice, and serve immediately on a bed of jasmine rice. *Serves 4.*

NOTE For a vegetarian version, replace the beef with cubed, firm tofu. Cook as for the beef, but remove the tofu before adding the rest of the ingredients. Spoon the tofu over the top before serving.

Ayam Manis (Sweet Balinese Chicken & Fish)

Sauce

2 teaspoons coriander seeds

1/4–1/3 cup peanut oil

3 onions, thinly sliced

2 cloves garlic, crushed or minced

2 stalks celery, chopped

1/4 cup Indian Curry Powder (page 23)

1 apple, coarsely chopped

1/3 cup golden raisins

Juice of 1 lime

3 ripe tomatoes, peeled

2 fresh red Thai chiles, seeded and coarsely chopped

1 stalk lemongrass, sliced into 1-inch lengths

3 tablespoons soy sauce

1 tablespoon ketjap manis *(available at Asian markets)*

1 3/4 cups coconut milk

4 boneless chicken breast halves (about 6–8 ounces each)

1/4 pound red snapper fillets, cut into strips

2 teaspoons Green Thai Chili Paste (page 24)

2 teaspoons crunchy peanut butter

2 teaspoons chopped fresh cilantro

1/3 cup sesame oil

3–4 cups rice, steamed

4 tablespoons chopped fresh chives

To make the sauce, dry roast the coriander in a small skillet over high heat, stirring occasionally, for about 2 minutes. Set aside. Combine the peanut oil, onions, garlic, and celery in a skillet over medium heat and sauté for 2–3 minutes. Add the Indian Curry Powder and cook for 2 minutes more. Stir in the remaining ingredients. Bring to a boil, then reduce heat and simmer for 30 minutes.

Preheat the oven to 400°F. With a meat mallet, pound the chicken breasts as thin as possible. Lay them out flat, and place an equal portion of fish, Green Thai Chili Paste, peanut butter, and cilantro in the center of each. Roll up the chicken to encase the filling and secure with toothpicks.

Heat the sesame oil in a skillet over high heat, add the chicken, and cook for 30 seconds on each side, or until golden brown. Drain on paper towels.

Put the chicken into a heavy casserole or clay pot. Pour the sauce over the chicken and cover. Bake for 30 minutes, or until the chicken is cooked through. Serve on a bed of steamed rice, garnished with the chives.

Serves 4.

Index